A Note From Denise Renner

The Word of God is so powerful in our lives. It is essential that every person spend time with God and study His Word in order to stay spiritually strong in these last days.

This study guide corresponds to my *TIME With Denise Renner* TV program by the same title that can be viewed at **deniserenner.org**. My desire is that through these lessons, you find the encouragement and freedom in Christ that you need. I believe the Holy Spirit is going to speak to you through the words you read in this study tool and that as you begin to use it, you will be *propelled* into the abundant life God has planned for you. I encourage you to make the effort to receive all He has for you and all He wants to do in you — it will definitely be worth it!

Whether you have walked with the Lord a long time or have just begun to follow Him, there is so much He wants to give you from His Word. He sees where you are, and He wants to meet you there.

> **Therefore do not worry about tomorrow, for tomorrow will worry about its own things. Sufficient for the day is its own trouble.**
> **— Matthew 6:34**

Your sister and friend in Jesus Christ,

Denise Renner

Denise Renner

The Love of God

Copyright © 2024 by Denise Renner
1814 W. Tacoma St.
Broken Arrow, Oklahoma 74012-1406

Published by Rick Renner Ministries
www.renner.org

ISBN 13: 978-1-6675-0926-6

ISBN 13 eBook: 978-1-6675-0927-3

TOPIC

The Love of God Revealed

SCRIPTURES

1. **Galatians 4:4** — But when the fullness of the time had come, God sent forth His Son, born of a woman, born under the law.

2. **Philippians 2:6-8** — Who, being in the form of God, did not consider it robbery to be equal with God, but made Himself of no reputation, taking the form of a bondservant, and coming in the likeness of men. And being found in appearance as a man, He humbled Himself and became obedient to the point of death, even the death of the cross.

3. **Hebrews 2:18** — For in that He Himself has suffered, being tempted, He is able to aid those who are tempted.

4. **Hebrews 4:15,16** — For we do not have a High Priest who cannot sympathize with our weaknesses, but was in all points tempted as we are, yet without sin. Let us therefore come boldly to the throne of grace, that we may obtain mercy and find grace to help in time of need.

5. **1 Corinthians 6:19,20** — Do you not know that your body is the temple of the Holy Spirit who is in you, whom you have from God, and you are not your own? For you were bought at a price; therefore glorify God in your body and in your spirit, which are God's.

6. **Colossians 2:15** — Having disarmed principalities and powers, He made a public spectacle of them, triumphing over them in it.

7. **Colossians 3:12** — Therefore, as the elect of God, holy and beloved, put on tender mercies, kindness, humility, meekness, longsuffering.

8. **John 3:16** — For God so loved the world that He gave His only begotten Son, that whoever believes in Him should not perish but have everlasting life.

SYNOPSIS

The five lessons in this study *The Love of God* will focus on the following topics:

- The Love of God Revealed
- The Love of God Displayed
- The Love of God Motivates
- The Love of God Pursues
- The Love of God Never Fails

The emphasis of this lesson:

God's unconditional love for us is so amazing! Out of His great love for us, God enacted a rescue plan: He sent His Son to Earth in the form of a humble servant. Jesus showed His love for us by laying down His life on the Cross to pay for our sin and then sent the Holy Spirit, with His great, unchanging, ever-present love, to dwell within us. We now know our true identity as His beloved children whom He wants to be with forever.

In this lesson, we are looking at something very exciting — the love of God. You may say, "I already know that God loves me. I've known that since I was five years old." The apostle Paul prayed in Ephesians 3:18 that we might know the "width and length and depth and height" of God's love. We can always know more than we do right now! Our revelation of God's great love for us can expand wider. So in this lesson, we are looking at the love of God that has been *revealed* to us.

God Opened the Curtain of Revelation on His Love

Imagine you are in a theater. You're sitting with the audience and expecting the play, ballet, or opera to begin. The curtain is drawn, and you're waiting for it to open. That's what God did; *He opened the curtain of revelation to us,* little by little.

We see the first opening of that curtain when we read about Adam and Eve in the Garden of Eden. They had wonderful fellowship with God, and they loved each other. Everything was so wonderful. Then Adam and Eve sinned, and God sent them out of the garden so they would not touch the Tree of Life and remain in that lost condition of sin forever.

Even in this fallen state, we see God's mercy revealed to them. When Adam and Eve were hiding from Him and covering themselves with leaves, God shed the first blood and covered them with the skin of animals. God made man, and man messed up, but God demonstrated His love and His rescuing, saving power.

The curtains were opened a little more as God revealed the Law. But men could not (and cannot) obey the Law. The Law was given to His children for their own good — to protect them from themselves — but in their own strength, they couldn't follow it.

Then God sent prophets, and a little more of God's love and mercy was revealed. The prophets were wonderful; they were a mouthpiece for God, and they did amazing things. They brought correction and wisdom to the people of Israel, and God's people continued to flourish. But they continued to stray from Him.

God Loved Us So Much That He Came in the Flesh

Galatians 4:4 says, "But when the fullness of the time had come, God sent forth His Son, born of a woman, born under the law." At just the right time, God sent Jesus — and we see the curtain opening. This is an amazing revelation; God loves us so much that He sent His Son to rescue us. Mankind kept messing up and sinning…God kept reaching out to mankind…mankind kept rejecting Him. So God said, in essence, "I've got to save them. I've got to get to them. I've sent My prophets. I've sent the Law. I'll just come Myself."

Jesus was God in the flesh! We see that all throughout the Bible — from Genesis to Revelation. God came to earth in the flesh. Think about this! We're talking about God Almighty, the Creator of Heaven and earth, who is giving you breath to breathe right now. He holds together every atom, proton, and neutron in this universe by His Word. He is the God who split the Red Sea and led the children of Israel through the desert to a place of freedom. He is the God who shut the mouths of the lions for Daniel, and He preserved Shadrach, Meshach, and Abednego in the fiery furnace.

That God — the Creator of the universe. *That* God — who loved you and me so much that He came to Earth. Yes, He was Jesus, but He was God. He was God in the flesh. And He came because of His great love for us.

Love Took on the Form of a Servant

Philippians 2:6-8 says, "Who, being in the form of God, did not consider it robbery to be equal with God, but made Himself of no reputation, taking the form of a bondservant, and coming in the likeness of men. And being found in appearance as a man, He humbled Himself and became obedient to the point of death, even the death of the cross." This amazing verse is talking about Jesus! God pulled back the curtain and showed us His great love for us when He stepped out of Heaven in the Person of Jesus Christ.

Again, Philippians 2:6 says that Jesus, "being in the form of God, did not consider it robbery to be equal with God." Yes, Jesus was God. But He set aside His godhood, His powerfulness — the power to split the Red Sea. Think about all the people who criticized Him, over and over again. The Pharisees said, "He casts out demons by Beelzebub, the ruler of the demons" (*see* Matthew 12:24). In His power, Jesus could have dealt with the Pharisees and all those who mocked Him like God had dealt with the rebellious people in the Old Testament. But Jesus had us on His heart. He was obedient to the Word and focused on the prize — our redemption.

When they tried to throw Jesus off the cliff, what if He had said, "Forget this!" He could have demonstrated the God kind of power, but Jesus wasn't holding on to that. He was holding onto *the form of a servant*. He was holding on to His humanness so He could understand us. This is so magnificent!

Powerful Love That Reaches Out To Rescue Us

Philippians 2:7 goes on to say, "But [Jesus] made Himself of no reputation, taking the form of a bondservant, and coming in the likeness of men." Why would God do this? You may be thinking, *If He made us, then surely He understands us.* But Scripture shows us *why* He did this.

Hebrews 2:18 says, "For in that He Himself has suffered, being tempted, He is able to aid those who are tempted." Jesus suffered and was tempted so He could help us when we are tempted. He came so He could understand us. Hebrews 4:15 and 16 says:

> **For we do not have a High Priest who cannot sympathize with our weaknesses, but was in all points tempted as we are, yet without sin. Let us therefore come boldly to the throne**

of grace, that we may obtain mercy and find grace to help in time of need.

We have a high priest who sympathizes with our weaknesses. How can He sympathize with our weaknesses? The Word says that He "was in all points tempted as we are, yet without sin" (Hebrews 4:16). In every single way we are tempted, He was tempted. He identifies with our weaknesses. He understands us. This is His love pulling back the curtain and revealing that He is not just the God who created the universe, but He is also the God who came to earth as a flesh-and-blood human. He was tempted just as we are tempted, and He overcame temptation — not as God but as a man.

Think for a moment about the Virgin Birth. God is so big, so mighty, and so powerful, yet He reduced Himself to a tiny embryo and was placed in the womb of a virgin named Mary. What kind of love is this? The Word of God goes on to say that He also "humbled Himself and became obedient to the point of death..." (Philippians 2:8). He went to the Cross to suffer for us — to take our place — and to take on our sin and guilt, our sickness and disease, doubt, hate, anger, jealousy, confusion, and anything that would come and bring destruction to the heart or the body of man. The love of God reached out through Jesus to rescue us from every sickness and disease and all sin.

This is a powerful love! And as we are studying His Word, the curtain is being drawn further and further apart, opening up to us this revelation of God's love to us *personally*. Jesus went so far as to die for us, to take our punishment, and to take our sin. But then He went further, and He gave us the Holy Spirit — our personal Counselor, Comforter, Helper, and Guide — to live inside us!

He Wants To Be With Us

When Jesus was talking to the disciples before His death, He said, in essence, "I need to go away now, but I'm sending Someone to you, and He'll be just like Me." You didn't get some kind of junior-size Holy Spirit to live inside you; you received *the* Holy Spirit, and He is exactly like Jesus. He came to live in *your* spirit, and He will never leave you. Oh, this is the love of God! He loves you so much. He wants to always be with you.

In the Old Testament, God dwelled in man-made temples to be near His people. The first temple was built in "a place that the Lord chose" (*see* Deuteronomy 12:5). It was the home of the Ark of the Covenant — the dwelling place of the Lord — and a place for His people to gather near Him. When that temple was destroyed, a second temple was built on the site of the original temple (*see* Ezra 1:1-4). But living in temples constructed of earthly materials was not God's desire. He said, in effect, "I didn't come to live in temples made of stone, but I came to live in your very body" (*see* Acts 17:24,25).

The apostle Paul shared the depth of His love in First Corinthians 6:19 and 20. In the *New International Version*, it says, "Do you not know that your bodies are temples of the Holy Spirit, who is in you, whom you have received from God? You are not your own; you were bought at a price. Therefore honor God with your bodies." If you're born again, you house within you the very Person of the Holy Spirit, who is just like Jesus. He loves you so much that He rescued you. He doesn't want to be apart from you, so He came to live within you. It's amazing!

Paul then shared another aspect of God's love for us. Colossians 2:15 says, "Having disarmed principalities and powers, He [Jesus] made a public spectacle of them, triumphing over them in it." Notice that word "disarmed." If you had a bomb and you didn't want it to go off, you would do something to turn off the bomb — so it couldn't go off. That's what Jesus did to the principalities and powers and the rulers of spiritual wickedness — He defeated them. He *disarmed* them — *made them powerless* — because of His immense love for us.

His Love Gives Us Our True Identity

Colossians 3:12 tells us that we are "the elect of God, holy and beloved." The love of God gives us our true identity. Your identity is not defined by what your parents say about you. It is not what your spouse might have said in an angry moment. Your identity is not determined by what a friend, teacher, sibling, or stranger says about you — your identity is *what God says about you.* This is the love of God. The "elect of God" is who you are (*see* Romans 8:33). You are holy. You are His beloved.

Maybe you've always wanted to be somebody's beloved. We all want that — we were created for relationship. We all want somebody to love us. Well, there's One who loves you and whose love will never change. *Never.* He won't give you the silent treatment. He won't judge you and put up a wall — like human love. No, His love is unconditional. He'll continue to love you and call you His beloved.

That's the love of God. The curtain has been opened to reveal this amazing truth: "God so loved the world that He gave His only begotten Son, that whoever believes in Him should not perish but have everlasting life" (John 3:16). He gave His life not so you would just have the promise of Heaven, but the Holy Spirit came so you could have abundant life *right now*. This is the most amazing love! He put His Holy Spirit, His very Person, right on the inside of you because He didn't want to live a second without your presence.

The Bible says that when we got saved, the Holy Spirit came in and put the very love of God in our heart, and it is with this unconditional love that we can love others (*see* Romans 5:5). He's done everything! Now we see the curtain completely pulled back, and we can discover even more about the magnificent power of the love of God. We can open our hearts to acknowledge and receive even more of this great love of God.

Isn't it amazing that we are loved so much? Even if we fail to do, say, or think the right thing, instead of pulling back from us or building a wall between us, God's unconditional love is constantly there. It has not changed. It does not move. It's there for us to open our heart and freely receive that magnificent love and forgiveness — again and again.

Oh, that we would understand this great love that's been given to us because we're in this together. We're one family. Those who are born again will spend eternity together. Forever and ever.

Father, we thank You for Your amazing love. We praise You! In the magnificent, wonderful name of Jesus. Amen.

STUDY QUESTIONS

Be diligent to present yourself approved to God, a worker who does not need to be ashamed, rightly dividing the word of truth.
— 2 Timothy 2:15

1. The love of God reached out through Jesus to rescue us from every sickness, disease, and all sin. Read First Peter 2:24; Colossians 1:13 and 14; First John 3:1; and Matthew 8:17. What do these passages reveal to you about God's great love for you?

2. In humility, love obeys and serves. Philippians 2:8 says, "And being found in appearance as a man, He humbled Himself and became obedient to the point of death, even the death of the cross." Notice how

humility and obedience go hand in hand. Where else do we see Jesus humbly serving out of love for others and obedience to the Father during His time on earth? (*Consider* John 13:1-17.)

3. In Ephesians 3:14-19, the apostle Paul prayed that we, being rooted and grounded in love, "may be able to comprehend with all the saints what is the width and length and depth and height — to know the love of Christ which passes knowledge...." What would happen if you prayed this prayer for yourself and your loved ones every day? What other prayers does the Bible record that Paul prayed? (*Consider* Ephesians 1:16-23; Colossians 1:9-14; Philippians 1:9-11.)

PRACTICAL APPLICATION

**But be doers of the word,
and not hearers only, deceiving yourselves.**
— James 1:22

1. In the program, Denise mentioned that your identity is not what your parents say, not what a spouse says, or what a friend, a teacher, a brother, or anybody else says — but your identity comes from *what God says about you.* This is the love of God. The "elect of God" is who you are. You are holy. You're beloved. Ephesians 1:6 says, "He made us accepted in the Beloved." You are *accepted* by God. Strip off the rejection you have felt from others and see yourself as *accepted* by God — because you are. Retreat to a quiet place and meditate on this profound truth! See yourself as *accepted* by God!

2. God's love for you is constant and it is pure. It's not earned based on your behavior and it does not change. It's simply there for you to receive. God's love is expressed through Jesus and what He did for you on the Cross. Read Isaiah 53:4 and 5. What do you perceive about God's great love? Write down what is being revealed to your heart about His love for you.

3. Take a moment to bask in His love and pray this from your heart: *Father, I thank You for Your magnificent love. Lord, by faith — not by my feelings, but by faith in the Word of God — I receive and acknowledge Your love. You, Father, love me unconditionally, and Your love does not change from day to day. It is always the same. It is constant, and I thank You for it. In Jesus' name. Amen.*

TOPIC

The Love of God Displayed

SCRIPTURES

1. **Galatians 4:4** — But when the fullness of the time had come, God sent forth His Son, born of a woman, born under the law.

2. **John 1:1-5** — In the beginning was the Word, and the Word was with God, and the Word was God. He was in the beginning with God. All things were made through Him, and without Him nothing was made that was made. In Him was life, and the life was the light of men. And the light shines in the darkness, and the darkness did not comprehend it.

3. **John 1:11** — He came to His own, and His own did not receive Him.

4. **John 1:14** — And the Word became flesh and dwelt among us, and we beheld His glory, the glory as of the only begotten of the Father, full of grace and truth.

5. **John 3:16** — For God so loved the world that He gave His only begotten Son, that whoever believes in Him should not perish but have everlasting life.

6. **Hebrews 1:3** — Who being the brightness of His glory and the express image of His person, and upholding all things by the word of His power, when He by Himself purged our sins, sat down at the right hand of the Majesty on high.

7. **Psalm 22:6-11** — But I am a worm, and no man; a reproach of men, and despised by the people. All those who see Me ridicule Me; they shoot out the lip, they shake the head, saying, "He trusted in the Lord, let Him rescue Him; let Him deliver Him, since He delights in Him!" But You are He who took Me out of the womb; You made Me trust while on My mother's breasts. I was cast upon You from birth. From My mother's womb You have been My God. Be not far from Me, for trouble is near; for there is none to help.

8. **Matthew 27:42,43** — "He saved others; Himself He cannot save. If He is the King of Israel, let Him now come down from the cross, and

we will believe Him. He trusted in God; let Him deliver Him now if He will have Him; for He said, 'I am the Son of God.'"

SYNOPSIS

The Bible reveals to us the great love of God for man. He loves us and wants relationship with us so much that He sent His Son, Jesus, to save us. His great love is on full display on the Cross. There, Jesus endured rejection, ridicule, agony, and the blasphemy of others to pay the full price for our sin. Because He loved us, we now have healing, deliverance, and forgiveness — and we can freely share these gifts with others, through His love that is shed abroad in our hearts.

The emphasis of this lesson:

The God who made the universe, the God who gives us breath to breathe, the God who can split the Red Sea — that very God came and died for us. Such humility is amazing! That's how much He loves us. He displayed His love through His actions, and as His beloved children, we are called to do likewise, through forgiving others and receiving what God has given us.

There's so much for us to learn about the *display* that God demonstrated for mankind to show us how much He loves us. People may say, "I love you," but truly, love is displayed *through action*. And what God did for us is complete. His actions show beyond a shadow of a doubt that He loves us, that He chose us, and that we are incredibly important to Him. We're so important to Him that He died for us. It's amazing.

A Display of Love Planned From the Beginning

As we unpack the meaning of the love of God displayed, let's look again at Galatians 4:4, which says, "But when the fullness of the time had come, God sent forth His Son, born of a woman, born under the law." There was a specific time that God was waiting for; a time when He would send forth His Son, born of a woman, born under the law. At that precise time, God said, "It's time. It's time that I rescue them Myself. They have sinned against Me and rejected Me. They can't fulfill My Law. They have rejected, stoned, and cursed My prophets. *I'm coming Myself.*"

This is such a great love that He has displayed to us! We should wake up every morning and say, "God, help me today to know how much You love me, and help me love others with the love that You've put inside me." This was God's plan from the beginning. John 1:1-5 says:

> **In the beginning was the Word, and the Word was with God, and the Word was God. He was in the beginning with God. All things were made through Him, and without Him nothing was made that was made. In Him was life, and the life was the light of men. And the light shines in the darkness, and the darkness did not comprehend it.**

These verses are talking about Jesus. In the very beginning, Jesus was with the Father and the Holy Spirit. Everything that has been made exists because of Him. Verse 5 says, "In Him was life, and the life was the light of men. And the light shines in the darkness, and the darkness did not comprehend it." There is no darkness so dark that God's light cannot overcome it.

Have you ever noticed that you can be in a dark room, but the minute you turn on the light, it expels the darkness? That's what Jesus did when He came into this world. He arrived at the perfect time. There was great darkness in the world, but when Jesus came, the Bible says, "In Him was life, and the life was the light of men" (1 John 1:5). He brought His light to this world.

The Heart of God Expressed in Action

But John 1:11 says, "He came to His own, and His own did not receive Him." Have you ever poured out your love to someone, only to have it rejected over and over again? Denise shared a story in her program about trying to befriend a woman many years ago. Denise said:

I tried to be a friend to her, but time and time again, she would just reject me and hurt my feelings. At that time, I didn't have many friends, so I kept forgiving her. But my love wasn't like God's love, because there came a point where I said, "I'm not going to forgive this person anymore" — because I didn't want to be hurt anymore. But that's not the God kind of love.

When God came to earth, He came to rescue. He came to rescue His own, but they didn't receive Him (*see* John 1:11). Instead, they rejected Him. Yet He *came* and He *gave*, knowing they would reject Him and not receive Him. But that is the love of God — the heart of God being expressed through Jesus. In Hebrews 1:3, it says that Jesus is the "express image" of God. What Jesus did is exactly what the Father would have done. What Jesus is doing today to rescue, save, heal, and do miracles is exactly what the Father is doing.

John 1:14 says, "And the Word became flesh and dwelt among us, and we beheld His glory, the glory as of the only begotten of the Father, full of grace and truth." Again, this is talking about Jesus, describing who He is and what He is like; He is full of grace and truth. Love doesn't just talk — love acts. God didn't just say, "I love you," and that's it. No, He said in John 3:16, "For God so loved the world that He gave His only begotten Son." When God said, "I love you," He came with a display of action, and that display of action was — and *is* — Jesus.

He Took on Ridicule

Psalm 22 shines a light on what Jesus went through on the Cross. These verses in the Bible reveal the feelings Jesus had and what it was like for Him as He took our sin, our sicknesses, our diseases, our poverty, our guilt, and our shame on the Cross.

Jesus said, "But I am a worm, and no man; a reproach of men, and despised by the people" (Psalm 22:6). These words convey His thoughts on the Cross. The word "worm" means *maggot*. Then Jesus said that He was "no man." In contrast, Jesus did not say, "I am an important man." These words here refer to an *unimportant* man. He was saying, in effect, "I am not important here." Jesus is the Creator of the universe, but He lowered Himself to such a place that on the Cross, He considered Himself to be as a worm; a man who had no importance.

Psalm 22:6 and 7 continue Jesus' cry from the Cross. He said, "…A reproach of men, and despised by the people. All those who see Me ridicule Me…." Have you ever been in a situation where the people all around you were ridiculing you or making fun of you? In the program, Denise shared a story about dealing with a situation like this when she was a young teenager and suffering from a horrible skin disease on her face:

> I was a teenager, and my face looked very, very bad because of a skin disease I had on my face. I would get skin treatments, but then it would look even worse. I remember one day when I went outside, and the other kids gathered in a circle around me. They sang a made-up song about me and made fun of me. They

mocked me and then said that I couldn't take a joke. I felt like I was nothing. But magnify that harassment a million times more to understand the weight of the ridicule that came upon Jesus on the Cross.

While Jesus was on the Cross, the demonic realm blasphemed him, made fun of Him, and put Him down. He was sinless, yet He submitted Himself to this punishment so we could be free from the ridicule and accusations. Jesus took upon Himself what rightfully belonged to us so we could be free. God lowered Himself to rescue us. He called Himself a worm and an unimportant man, while everyone around Him ridiculed Him.

He Didn't Try To Rescue Himself

Then Jesus said, "They shoot out the lip, they shake the head, saying, 'He trusted in the Lord, let Him rescue Him; let Him deliver Him, since He delights in Him!'" (Psalm 22:7,8). Matthew 27:42 and 43 paints the picture of what this looked like. Jesus was on the Cross, and the religious leaders were screaming about Him, saying, "He saved others; Himself He cannot save. If He is the King of Israel, let Him now come down from the cross, and we will believe Him. He trusted in God; let Him deliver Him now if He will have Him; for He said, 'I am the Son of God.'"

That's what they said about Jesus as He was suffering and hanging from the nails that pierced His hands and feet — suffering for them; for their forgiveness and their salvation. He was hanging on that Cross for them and for us! Yet they were ridiculing Him and blaspheming Him, saying, in essence, "Come on, Jesus, save Yourself! Cry out to God if He'll hear You. You said He was Your Father."

But Jesus didn't come off that Cross. He didn't yell back at His accusers, "Don't you curse Me!" Jesus willingly laid down His life for us. The Bible tells us that when the chief priests came to arrest Jesus, Peter cut off a servant's ear trying to protect Jesus (*see* John 18:10). But Jesus, with compassion, put the man's ear back on — a miracle! Jesus then said to Peter, "Put your sword in its place, for all who take the sword will perish by the sword. Or do you think that I cannot now pray to My Father, and He will provide Me with more than twelve legions of angels?" (Matthew 26:52,53). They didn't take Jesus' life — Jesus *gave* His life for us. It was the love of God being *displayed* that day.

Forgive as He Has Forgiven You

Jesus continued, "But You are He who took Me out of the womb; You made Me trust while on My mother's breasts. I was cast upon You from birth. From My mother's womb You have been My God. Be not far from Me, for trouble is near; for there is none to help" (Psalm 22:9-11). Here, Jesus is describing His communion and fellowship with His Father.

When Jesus was on the Cross, Matthew 27:46 tells us that He cried out with a loud voice, saying, "My God, My God, why have You forsaken Me?" Jesus was the Son of Man though He was fully God, but He put aside His godhood and He died for us. He refused to call legions of angels to rescue Him from the Cross — He willingly laid down His life for you and me.

That sacrifice is His love displayed and it paid the debt owed for our sin. Paid in full — we are forgiven! So there is no excuse for any of us *not* to forgive others! We don't have the right to say, "I know You've forgiven me, Lord, but I can't forgive them!" He forgave us and He paid the complete price to put the love of God inside us so *we* could freely forgive.

His Perfect Love Casts Out All Fear

Jesus took every sickness and disease, every torment of our mind, and every pain in our body. He took it upon Himself on the Cross. He was scorned, spit upon, humiliated, shamed, and ridiculed. He was lied about, falsely accused, hated, and denied. He was even betrayed by one of His closest friends. Yet He went to the Cross — for all of us.

The love of God on display that day was (and still is) so perfect that *all* fear was cast out. Fear lost its power that day, so it does not have any power or authority over you, because the perfect love of God, which He displayed and put inside you, casts out fear (*see* 1 John 4:18).

This display of God's love is so great that when we believe His Word, His power comes to us and gives us the ability to forgive any offender of any offense. It gives us the power to believe His Word and trust Him to heal any sickness or disease that we may encounter and offer mercy and understanding and patience in every situation. In displaying His love, He gave us the power to express the love of God that's in our hearts because of what He did for us on the Cross.

Receive What His Love Has Paid For

God didn't save us just so we could go to Heaven (even though Heaven will be magnificent). He dwells inside us so we can have a relationship with Him and He can reach others through us.

Jesus paid the complete price — not a partial payment — to save us from hell and ourselves. The love He displayed paid the complete, 100-percent price, once and for all. When Jesus died on the Cross, He said, "It is finished," which means it is *paid for in full.* He paid for it — salvation, healing, deliverance, forgiveness, freedom from sin…all of it — and it's ours to freely receive.

Imagine if somebody gave you a $2 million house, and they said, "Here it is. It's for you. All you have to do is receive it." If you say, "I don't know if I can receive it. I didn't pay for it. I didn't earn it," you will not receive that house. But if you say, "I receive your gift," then you'll receive it — that beautiful home is yours!

It's the same with the love of God. As you say to Him, "Lord, I receive everything that You have paid for," you receive it! Receive it now. Declare, "I receive my healing. I receive forgiveness. I receive Your powerful love inside me to love and forgive others as I've been loved and forgiven. Thank You for Your power of the love You displayed. I receive it now by faith. In Jesus' name. Amen."

STUDY QUESTIONS

Be diligent to present yourself approved to God, a worker who does not need to be ashamed, rightly dividing the word of truth.
— 2 Timothy 2:15

1. Hebrews 12:1 and 2 says, "…Let us run with endurance the race that is set before us, looking unto Jesus, the author and finisher of our faith, *who for the joy that was set before Him endured the cross,* despising the shame, and has sat down at the right hand of the throne of God." *You* were the "joy set before Him" when He endured the Cross. That's how much He loves you. What other scriptures reveal His great love for you? (*Consider* John 3:16,17; and First John 3:1.)

2. Read Romans 8:35-39. Is there anything that can separate you from the love of Christ? According to verse 37, what makes you more than a conqueror in every situation?

3. John 3:16 speaks of God's love toward you. What kind of love does First John 3:16 speak of?

PRACTICAL APPLICATION

**But be doers of the word,
and not hearers only, deceiving yourselves.
—James 1:22**

1. In the program, Denise encouraged us to pray this prayer daily: *God, help me to know how much You love me today, and help me love others with the love that You've put inside me.* Matthew 22:39 says, "You shall love your neighbor as yourself." What can you do this week to extend the love of God to your neighbor?

2. This is love displayed: Jesus paid the complete price to put the love of God inside you so you could freely receive His forgiveness *and* forgive others. Is there someone you have not forgiven? Realize that the Lord has forgiven you of everything, and He placed the ability to forgive inside you. Take a moment to pray and forgive this person of the debt he or she owes you.

3. The God who made the universe, who gives us breath and split the Red Sea — that very God sent Jesus to die for you. The favorite chorus says, "...Yes, Jesus loves me. Yes, Jesus loves me. Yes, Jesus loves me, the Bible tells me so." Sing that simple children's song and allow that profound truth to permeate your heart and soul.

LESSON 3

TOPIC

The Love of God Motivates

SCRIPTURES

1. **Psalm 22:6-11** — But I am a worm, and no man; a reproach of men, and despised by the people. All those who see Me ridicule

Me; they shoot out the lip, they shake the head, saying, "He trusted in the Lord, let Him rescue Him; let Him deliver Him, since He delights in Him!" But You are He who took Me out of the womb; You made Me trust while on My mother's breasts. I was cast upon You from birth. From My mother's womb You have been My God. Be not far from Me, for trouble is near; for there is none to help.

2. **Psalm 22:12-18** — Many bulls have surrounded Me; strong bulls of Bashan have encircled Me. They gape at Me with their mouths, like a raging and roaring lion. I am poured out like water, and all My bones are out of joint; my heart is like wax; it has melted within Me. My strength is dried up like a potsherd, and My tongue clings to My jaws; You have brought Me to the dust of death. For dogs have surrounded Me; the congregation of the wicked has enclosed Me. They pierced My hands and My feet; I can count all My bones. They look and stare at Me. They divide My garments among them, and for My clothing they cast lots.

3. **1 Corinthians 6:19,20** — Or do you not know that your body is the temple of the Holy Spirit who is in you, whom you have from God, and you are not your own? For you were bought at a price; therefore glorify God in your body and in your spirit, which are God's.

4. **1 John 4:4** (*KJV*) — Ye are of God, little children, and have overcome them: because greater is he that is in you, than he that is in the world.

5. **Philippians 2:13** — For it is God who works in you both to will and to do for His good pleasure.

SYNOPSIS

When we are born again, the love of God is fully shed abroad in our hearts by the Holy Ghost. We only need to look at the Cross to see how powerful His love is. It is through His love that He poured Himself out completely, giving His all *for us*. That love now dwells inside us — those who call Him Lord and Savior — motivating us to put aside selfish ways and act in love, which honors Him.

The emphasis of this lesson:

We can love others and forgive as He has forgiven because of God's great love within us. As we come to recognize and understand the amazing depth, length, breadth, and height of His love that we carry within

us, we become empowered to take action and live for Him, motivated by His love to be just like Him in everything we do.

In Lesson 1 and 2, we examined the love of God being revealed and the love of God being displayed. Now let's look at the love of God as the great motivator. The more we know about the love of God and how much He loves us, the more it motivates us to love like He loves and honor Him through our actions and good deeds. Through the new birth, the love of God has been poured out in our hearts by the Holy Ghost — not a "junior-size" love of God, but the very love of God in its fullness. Knowing and understanding His love for us is a great motivator in our lives. We can love and forgive others because of the huge price that Jesus paid for us.

The Great Exchange of Forgiveness

On the program, Denise shared the testimony of a dear friend who had the power to forgive someone because she was motivated by the love of God. This woman had fallen in love and married who she thought was the love of her life, but the man began to mistreat her. He joined the army and never communicated with her or their daughter. He never sent them any money and acted like they didn't exist.

When her husband was discharged from the army, he prospered financially and moved in with another woman, but he never contacted his wife, reached out to his daughter, or helped them financially in any way. His actions caused her great pain. Sometimes she would feel hatred toward her husband, or she would feel shame about how he treated her and her daughter. She didn't know what to do.

But then she was introduced to Jesus, and she received Him into her heart. She started studying about the love of God and what Jesus did for her on the Cross. She came to understand the price He paid for the forgiveness of her sin, and she realized she needed to give that same forgiveness to her husband. She wasn't trying to get money or regain their relationship. Her desire to forgive her husband was about her relationship with Jesus.

So this woman reached out to her husband because she knew she could not live with this unforgiveness and offense in her heart. She realized she wasn't going to be able to move forward in her life if she did not forgive him, so she decided to do something radical. She went to his home with a bucket of water and a towel and knelt at his feet.

He said, "What are you doing?" She responded, "I'm going to wash your feet." And he said, "You're not going to wash my feet until I wash yours." At that moment, there was a great exchange of forgiveness and acceptance of one another, and she completely forgave him. Jesus' love is a great motivator!

Forgiveness Brought Restoration to This Family

The love of God is so great that it motivated this woman to do the unthinkable — washing her estranged husband's feet. This man had betrayed her; he was an adulterer, he never gave her any financial support, nor did he recognize his daughter's existence. Yet this woman forgave him, and in response, he washed her feet — there was a great exchange of forgiveness.

But the story doesn't end there. Soon after that encounter, the man died. At the funeral, instead of feeling bitterness, depression, shame, hate, and rejection, she felt love and forgiveness for this man. Friend, the love of God is miracle-working!

God's love is like a bulldozer that bulldozes through pain and unforgiveness and the "You owe me, and I'll never forgive you" attitude. It plows right through the hate and separates what's true from what's not true. The love of God is a great motivator. It motivated Denise's friend to do the radical thing and forgive, which brought healing and restoration to that family.

Jesus Endured Ridicule and Shame for Our Sake

Let's revisit Psalm 22, which reveals the thoughts and feelings Jesus had on the Cross. Jesus said, "I am a worm, and no man" (v. 6), which means, "I am not an important man." This passage of Scripture goes on to say that Jesus expressed that He was "a reproach of men, and despised by the people," and they ridiculed Him. He continued, "…They shoot out the lip, they shake the head, saying 'He trusted in the Lord, let Him rescue Him; let Him deliver Him, since He delights in Him!'" (vv. 7,8). Matthew 27 testifies to what was prophesied in Psalm 22 — the slander and venom that was hurled at Jesus by the religious leaders. Jesus endured this on the Cross out of His great love for you and me.

Psalm 22:9-11 goes on to say, "But You are He who took Me out of the womb; You made Me trust while on My mother's breasts. I was cast upon

You from birth. From My mother's womb, You have been My God. Be not far from Me, for trouble is near; for there is none to help." These verses show Jesus' relationship with His Father and how He was there when Jesus was born. This was all going through Jesus' mind while He was on the Cross.

Jesus' words continue, "Many bulls have surrounded Me; strong bulls of Bashan have encircled Me. They gape at Me with their mouths, like a raging and roaring lion" (Psalm 22:12,13). The region of Bashan was famous for the quality of its livestock; the cows were very large, and the bulls were very strong and powerful. This verse is a picture of the religious leaders that surrounded Jesus; they had power, clout, and authority. These priests were like raging, roaring lions, pressing on Jesus with their rejection, ridicule, and strength, and using their power and influence to demean and blaspheme Him. Again, Psalm 22 gives us insight into what Jesus went through for us.

When Peter chopped off the ear of that servant in the Garden of Gethsemane the night before Jesus was crucified, Jesus picked up the ear, healed the man, and said, in essence, "Peter, put away your sword. Can I not call legions of angels right now to save Me?" Jesus knew exactly how He would die because it had been prophesied. He knew they would ridicule and blaspheme Him. He knew they would strip Him. He knew He'd be betrayed. He knew, but He said *yes* to the Cross because He loves us.

He Poured Himself Out Completely

Psalm 22 continues to reveal Jesus' thoughts on the Cross: "I am poured out like water" (v. 14). We cannot even begin to imagine the amount of His blood that was being shed. In the movie, *The Passion of the Christ*, the chastisement and crucifixion scenes are so horrendous that they are difficult to recount, yet the film still falls short of depicting what Jesus looked like. Isaiah 52:14 states that He was unrecognizable as a man. His blood was poured out like water from the wounds that covered His body.

The whip that was used to beat Jesus had metal and glass attached to the ends of each of the multiple, leather straps. And when the cords wrapped around His body — His face, His chest, and His legs — every piece of jagged metal, glass, and bone attached itself to His skin. It gashed His skin, down to His muscles and sinews. His blood poured from Him like *water*.

Verse 14 goes on to say, "And all My bones are out of joint." We cannot even imagine the pain that this brought upon our Savior. Have you ever had a bone out of joint? It is so painful! Jesus said, "*All* my bones are out of joint." Then the verse continues, "My heart is like wax; it has melted within Me." One commentator said that it was like there was just no more strength in Him. As His body hung on the nails in His hands and feet, He grew weary and had no more resistance. His heart "melted" like wax. Again, this is what Jesus endured because of His love for us.

Psalm 22 continues, "My strength is dried up like a potsherd, and My tongue clings to My jaws. You have brought Me to the dust of death. For dogs have surrounded Me; the congregation of the wicked has enclosed Me. They pierced My hands and My feet; I can count all My bones. They look and stare at Me. They divide My garments among them, and for My clothing they cast lots" (vv. 15-18).

Jesus did this for us. This display of His love was not to make us feel bad, but it's a great motivator when we look at what He did. It motivates us to love and to forgive. It spurs us to love like He loves because the love of God has been "shed abroad in our hearts by the Holy Ghost" (Romans 5:5 *KJV*).

Love Like He Loves

We're *all* tempted by our selfish ways. But as we truly grasp what Jesus did in laying down His life for us, it motivates us to put our selfish ways aside and love like He loves and forgive like He forgives. Do you believe in your heart and confess with your mouth that Jesus is Lord — that He died on the Cross, was buried, and God raised Him from the dead? Then you are forgiven, and you *can* love like He loves and forgive like He forgives!

Do you know who now lives in you? First Corinthians 6:19 and 20 reveals, "Or do you not know that your body is the temple of the Holy Spirit who is in you, whom you have from God, and you are not your own? For you were bought at a price; therefore glorify God in your body and in your spirit, which are God's." When we recognize the love of God that has been deposited inside us, we are motivated to love and forgive, just as that love motivated Denise's friend to forgive her husband.

God wants to live through you. He wants to heal through you because He lives in you. He wants to serve through you and touch the brokenhearted with the love of God that is in you. This is so powerful!

Scriptures like Philippians 4:13, which says, "I can do all things through Christ who strengthens me," make perfect sense because of what His love has done. If love did that — *and it did* — then if we trust in Christ, we *can* do all things through Him! First John 4:4 in the *King James Version* declares, "…Greater is he that is in you, than he that is in the world." The Greater One *lives* in you!

Who is the Greater One? The Holy Spirit! The love of God that He put in your heart is greater than any offense or anything else that has tried to come against you and bring you down. The One who lives inside you is greater. Philippians 2:13 says, "For it is God who works in you both to will and to do for His good pleasure." The love of God is the great motivator to get us to do His will and His pleasure. It's God working in us. It's *His* love working inside us.

His Love Is Alive Within Us

The Word of God is so powerful. Hebrews 4:12 says, "The word of God is living and powerful, and sharper than any two-edged sword, piercing even to the division of soul and spirit, and of joints and marrow, and is a discerner of the thoughts and intents of the heart." It's the Word of God that opens up our motives and shows us the intent of our heart. His love is a great motivator for us to love more, forgive more, and believe more — because Jesus has already done it. He did everything for us!

As Psalm 22 reveals, Jesus suffered greatly for us. It would be one thing for *us* to suffer because we're not without sin. But Jesus *was* sinless; He was the Spotless Lamb. And He volunteered for that death and that suffering. He did it because He loves you. God loves you, and He didn't want to be without you. He didn't want to be separated from you for one second. That's why He sent the Holy Spirit to live inside you. This is the love of God — the great motivator.

STUDY QUESTIONS

Be diligent to present yourself approved to God, a worker who does not need to be ashamed, rightly dividing the word of truth.
— 2 Timothy 2:15

1. The love of God is miracle-working! It's like a bulldozer that plows through pain, unforgiveness, hate, and the attitude, *You owe me, and*

I'll never forgive you. When you allow His love to flow through you to others, *victory* comes. What do the first three words in First Corinthians 13:8 say about love? What kinds of victories might you see if you'll yield to His great love?

2. As we see what Jesus did on the Cross, it causes us to put aside our selfish ways, love like He loves, and forgive like He forgives. What He did for us was done on purpose, and it leads us to intentionally extend love and forgiveness to others. What can we learn about forgiving others by looking at Stephen's response in Acts 7:54-60?

3. Galatians 5:6 (*AMPC*) describes how faith is "activated and energized and expressed and working through love." If your faith isn't working, check up on your love walk. Take inventory: Are you extending the love of God to those around you? If not, make the necessary adjustments now, and watch your faith soar!

PRACTICAL APPLICATION

But be doers of the word,
and not hearers only, deceiving yourselves.
— James 1:22

1. Psalm 22:14 says, "I am poured out like water." It's hard to imagine the amount of blood that poured from Jesus as He was scourged and then crucified. Jesus poured out His love in a tangible way when He died on the Cross for you. He did it in your place. Take time to meditate on the fact that His blood literally poured out like water — for *you. Receive* His love and *respond* to it with a grateful heart. Sincerely *thank* Him for all He did for you. You may even want to *write* a heartfelt love letter of gratitude to Him.

2. Each of us faces challenges, but we must be aware of the needs of others and be a vehicle by which God can minister to them. Denise mentioned in the program that God "wants to touch the brokenhearted." Psalm 147:3 says, "He heals the brokenhearted and binds up their wounds." And often He uses *people* to do that. Who do you know that is brokenhearted? Ask God how you can be an extension of His love and bring healing to them today.

3. Did God minister to your heart as you read the testimony about forgiveness? Is there someone you've held a grudge against because of the way that person treated you? Today is the day to let go of that offense.

What happened to you may have been terrible, but the love of God that was poured out for you empowers you to let it go and be free of that offense. You are forgiven, and He wants *you* to be free from the trap of unforgiveness and offense. Take a moment to pray, releasing that person and freeing yourself of the offense. *Lord, I forgive* [insert name]. *It's with the power of Your love that I can forgive* [insert name] *and release myself of this offense. In Jesus' name. Amen.*

TOPIC

The Love of God Pursues

SCRIPTURES

1. **Matthew 5:43-48** — "You have heard that it was said, 'You shall love your neighbor and hate your enemy.' But I say to you, love your enemies, bless those who curse you, do good to those who hate you, and pray for those who spitefully use you and persecute you, that you may be sons of your Father in heaven; for He makes His sun rise on the evil and on the good, and sends rain on the just and on the unjust. For if you love those who love you, what reward have you? Do not even the tax collectors do the same? And if you greet your brethren only, what do you do more than others? Do not even the tax collectors do so? Therefore you shall be perfect, just as your Father in heaven is perfect."

2. **Romans 5:5** *(KJV)* — ...The love of God is shed abroad in our hearts by the Holy Ghost which is given unto us.

3. **1 Corinthians 14:1** — Pursue love....

4. **Romans 14:19** — Therefore let us pursue the things which make for peace and the things by which one may edify another.

5. **1 John 4:7-10** — Beloved, let us love one another, for love is of God; and everyone who loves is born of God and knows God. He who does not love does not know God, for God is love. In this the love of God was manifested toward us, that God has sent His only begotten Son into the world, that we might live through Him. In this is love, not

that we loved God, but that He loved us and sent His Son to be the propitiation for our sins.

6. **1 John 4:18** — There is no fear in love; but perfect love casts out fear, because fear involves torment....

SYNOPSIS

In His great love, God forgave us, even when we were far from Him due to sin. Now that we are born again and His love is shed abroad in our heart, He calls on us to love and forgive others — even our enemies. Without His help, this would be impossible. But because His unfailing love dwells within us, we can draw upon Him to love others as He has loved us.

The emphasis of this lesson:

The Word of God makes it clear that we are called to love others and to forgive them, just as we have been forgiven. As we allow His love to motivate and empower us to forgive our enemies, His love sets us free from fear and torment. In Christ, we are not victims but victors — overcoming victoriously through Him who loves us.

There's nothing bigger in this world than the love of God. It's this love that compelled Him to step out of Heaven and into this world to save us. The magnificent love of God came to earth in the package of a little baby born in Bethlehem. What a miracle! What a gift! And He did this because His love for us is so great!

A High-Level Love

In this lesson, we'll dig a little deeper into the love of God to discover how we can truly love our enemies. You may say, "I don't know how I can love my enemies. You don't know what they've done." But when Jesus said that we are to love our enemies, it wasn't just a suggestion. Matthew 5:43-45 says,

> **You have heard that it was said, "You shall love your neighbor and hate your enemy." But I say to you, love your enemies, bless those who curse you, do good to those who hate you, and pray for those who spitefully use you and persecute you, that you may be sons of your Father in heaven; for He makes His sun**

rise on the evil and on the good, and sends rain on the just and on the unjust.

God wants us to love those who are good, those who are bad, those who are just, and those who are unjust because God brings rain on them, just as He brings rain on us. Look now at the rest of that passage of Scripture, Matthew 5:46-48:

> **For if you love those who love you, what reward have you? Do not even the tax collectors do the same? And if you greet your brethren only, what do you do more than others? Do not even the tax collectors do so? Therefore you shall be perfect, just as your Father in heaven is perfect.**

The Word of God has a lot to say about *why* we should love, and it also reveals that the Holy Spirit lives inside of us, which *equips* us to love like He loves — even our enemies. Even if they persecute us and despitefully use us, we are to love them. He is saying we are to love everyone. This is a high-level love that Jesus is teaching about.

His Love Is Greater

Jesus asked if we love only those who love us, then how is our love any more special than the love the tax collectors offered? Tax collectors were horrible to the people they were appointed to serve. They collected more taxes than needed and kept some for themselves. People hated the tax collectors because they were traitors to their own people.

Imagine the fear and hate that was in the people's hearts when they heard the words, "Give me your taxes. You owe them now." Then the tax collectors would add an additional amount that they wanted for themselves. And the person they were demanding payment from was required to pay the amount. It was a terrible situation. Yet Jesus said about these men, "Even *they* are kind to those who are kind to them."

Jesus asked some penetrating questions! But we may wonder how we can love someone who hurts us and treats us poorly. What if that person does wrong to us over and over again? What if that person lies about us or treats us with contempt? How are we supposed to love him or her? How can this be possible? The answer is found in the love of God.

God's Love Is in Our Heart

In her program, Denise shared about a time many years ago when she found herself in an unexpected position and had to reach out to the Lord for help. She said:

> Many, many years ago, before I was married to Rick, I was accused by one of my relatives of doing something I did not do. But this relative believed it, and she gossiped about me. That relative told another relative, who then told another relative. And finally, a relative told my sister and my sister told me.
>
> I said, "That is absolutely ridiculous," and I laughed. But the more I thought about it, the more it hurt. I thought, *That is really ugly of them to gossip about me and to believe something horrible about me.* It hurt because I loved my relatives. I only got to see them once a year, but I cherished the time I had with them. This experience brought something ugly into my heart toward my relatives. I wondered how I could face them when I saw them again. How could I face them and talk to them when they believed such ugly things about me?
>
> I felt like I was in a prison! And I asked the Lord, "How am I going to love my relatives now?" Of course, I knew what He was going to say. The Lord told me, "You have to forgive them." And through the power of God's love in me, I *did* forgive them.

Jesus made it clear that we are to love and bless our enemies (*see* Matthew 5:44). But how can we do that? Romans 5 reveals the good news! It says, "…The love of God has been poured out in our hearts by the Holy Spirit who was given to us" (Romans 5:5). God's love — the love that He loves Jesus with, and the love that He loves us with — was poured out in our heart by the Holy Spirit when we were born again. God is not asking you to do something that you don't have the equipment to do. You *do* have the equipment! If you are born again, *the very love of God is in your heart.*

Purpose in Your Heart To Pursue Love and Peace

You might say, "Okay, I have the love of God. That's really good. But *how* am I to love my enemies and those who despitefully use me?" First Corinthians 14:1 presents a simple truth. The verse starts, "Pursue love…." The word "pursue" is the same word that's found in Romans 14:19, where it says we are to "pursue the things which make for peace." This word translated "pursue" is the Greek word *dioko*, which means *to be on the hunt*. In other words, it is something we do *intentionally* and *on purpose*, and it does not depend on our feelings. Again, First Corinthians 14:19 says we are to "pursue love…." We must purpose in our heart *to follow after* and *be on the hunt* for love.

If love doesn't well up inside you for that person, then how will you be able to give love? You *pursue* it — you purpose in your heart to love. Maybe you don't "feel" love for that person, but it doesn't matter because the love of God inside you is eternal and far greater than your natural feelings. Your feelings and thoughts can change (even your enemy can change), but the love of God inside you cannot and will not change. He is constant; His love is constant.

So we must pursue others with the love that's inside us. We must purpose in our heart to agree with that love and to give that love to the enemy, even to those who despitefully use and gossip about us. We're going to pursue them with the love of God that is within us. That's powerful! And how will we guard our heart? How will we keep fear out of our heart? We keep fear *out* of our heart by keeping the love of God *in* our heart!

Have you ever seen hunters or known people who hunt? They put on clothes that blend in with the grass and trees. If they are hunting deer, they may sit up in the trees for hours, absolutely silent, waiting for a deer to come into range. Everything hunters do, they do on purpose. That's what the Word of God is telling us to do. We must purpose in our heart to love — to acknowledge the love inside us, and, on purpose, freely give His love to that person. Hunters don't accidentally end up in that tree; they make a plan and prepare to be there. And we need to be just as intentional with the love of God.

Empowered To Love Our Enemies

In Matthew 5, Jesus instructed us to love our enemies. Let's dig a little deeper into how we can do this by taking a look at First John 4:7-10, which says,

> **Beloved, let us love one another, for love is of God; and every-
> one who loves is born of God and knows God. He who does
> not love does not know God, for God is love. In this the love
> of God was manifested toward us, that God has sent His only**

begotten Son into the world, that we might live through Him. In this is love, not that we loved God, but that He loved us and sent His Son to be the propitiation for our sins.

We're not under pressure to love. We can't make ourselves love, nor can we produce love by ourselves. The love within us comes from the love of God that's in our spirit. And it's not about our love for God — it's that God loved us first. When we understand this truth, it makes us *want* to love because we know that the Lover — the Holy Spirit inside us — is the source of that love. He empowers us to love our enemies and those who may despitefully use us, gossip about us, or hurt us.

But always remember that God loves *you*. The Holy Spirit inside you loves you like no one on earth could ever love you. His love is infinite, unconditional, and perfect. *You are loved!*

We Love Because We Have God on the Inside

Let's look at Jesus' life. Jesus never said, "If those Pharisees curse me, accuse me, or try to kill me one more time, then that's it. I'm not doing this anymore." Because He was walking in the love of God, Jesus was able to love the unlovely. And you have Jesus dwelling inside you, so *you* can love the unlovely.

Jesus — who lives in you — has given you the power to love. Even if someone hurts you one day and again the next day, you have the power inside you to love, forgive, and bless that person. The love in you is greater than any pressure around you in this world that would try to convince you to give up on that love.

Matthew 27:39 and 40 says, "…Those who passed by blasphemed Him, wagging their heads and saying, 'You who destroy the temple and build it in three days, save Yourself! If You are the Son of God, come down from the cross.'" Jesus didn't come off the cross when they blasphemed Him. He never gave up!

They blasphemed Him, ridiculed Him, and put Him down. They treated Him meanly and said, "He saved others; Himself He cannot save. If He is the King of Israel, let Him now come down from the cross, and we will believe Him. He trusted in God; let Him deliver Him now if He will have Him; for He said, 'I am the Son of God'" (Matthew 27:42,43). Yet Jesus said, "Father, forgive them, for they do not know what they do" (Luke 23:34).

Why is this so important? Because Jesus loved His enemies, and He told us to love our enemies. So we *can* love our enemies.

Jesus gave us the Holy Spirit and the love of God to dwell within us. First John 4:20 says, "…He who does not love his brother whom he has seen, how can he love God whom he has not seen?" He is admonishing us and teaching us that we have all we need — the love of God inside us — to love our enemy and those who hurt us and forgive them.

Not Victims, but Victors in Christ

Why should you walk in love? Why should you love your enemies? There is tremendous freedom in love, because "perfect love casts out fear" (1 John 4:18). When you walk in the love of God, you choose to be the victor, not the victim. Jesus wasn't a victim on the Cross; He was — and *is* — the Victor. He reigns victorious and He is the picture of love that gives until the very end. He said, "It is finished" (John 19:30). He paid the price. He is our Perfect Example.

Jesus gave us everything we need. When we became born again, He put the love of God — the Holy Spirit — inside us, so we could love our enemies and bless those who despitefully use us. We are equipped to forgive because of the love of God inside us and Jesus' finished work on the Cross.

We can remain free instead of being bound up in fear, thinking, *What if this person says this? What if they do that? What if this is not fair?* Such thoughts do not bring any peace to your heart, but God's love casts out *all* fear.

Again, First John 4:18 says, "There is no fear in love; but perfect love casts out fear, because fear involves torment." There's no torment with God. Jesus was tormented on the Cross for us so that we could have His perfect love and give that perfect love to others. We are not victims — we are victors! In Him, we can overcome anything the world may throw at us. In Him, we are free to act in faith, love others, and forgive, all without fear. What a glorious gift we have in the love of God!

STUDY QUESTIONS

Be diligent to present yourself approved to God, a worker
who does not need to be ashamed, rightly dividing the word of truth.
— 2 Timothy 2:15

1. When you forgive those who have wronged you, you free them! Read Matthew 18:21-35. Why is it important to forgive from your heart? (*Consider* Matthew 18:35.)

2. In the program, Denise asked, "How are we going to guard our heart? How are we going to keep fear out of our heart?" And she shared the answer, "By the love of God that is *in* our heart!" What does Proverbs 4:23 (*AMPC*) reveal about the importance of guarding your heart?

3. The Lord forgave you of everything. What is an appropriate response to His great forgiveness? (*Consider* Psalm 103:1-5.)

PRACTICAL APPLICATION

But be doers of the word,
and not hearers only, deceiving yourselves.
— James 1:22

1. The love of God pursues. Romans 14:19 says, "Therefore let us pursue the things which make for peace and the things by which one may edify another." We are to pursue others with the love that's inside us. How? By purposing to agree with that love and giving that love to others. Who can you pursue with God's love? Ask the Lord to lead you in the best way to be a channel of His love to that person.

2. Thank God for the power of the Holy Spirit who is in you! His power and His great love inside you are being revealed even as you read this study guide. Right now, by faith, release, forgive, and choose on purpose to love those who have despitefully used you. You can love your enemies in the precious and powerful name of Jesus and by His Holy Spirit who lives in you. Pray, *Lord, I choose to love my enemies, and those who have despitefully used me. In Jesus' name. Amen.*

3. While it is important to love and forgive those who have wronged you, if you are in a dangerous situation in your marriage or another relationship, it's essential to get to a place of safety — and ensure your children are safe as well. If you are in an emotionally or physically

abusive relationship, reach out to a pastor, counselor, or domestic violence hotline and devise a safety plan to ensure your protection and overall well-being.

TOPIC

The Love of God Never Fails

SCRIPTURES

1. **1 John 4:8** — He who does not love does not know God, for God is love.

2. **1 Corinthians 13:8** — Love never fails....

3. **1 Corinthians 13:13** — And now abide faith, hope, love, these three; but the greatest of these is love.

4. **Hebrews 1:10-12** — "You, Lord, in the beginning laid the foundation of the earth, and the heavens are the work of Your hands. They will perish, but You remain; and they will all grow old like a garment; like a cloak You will fold them up, and they will be changed. But You are the same, and Your years will not fail."

5. **John 20:5-7** — And he, stooping down and looking in, saw the linen cloths lying there; yet he did not go in. Then Simon Peter came, following him, and went into the tomb; and he saw the linen cloths lying there, and the handkerchief that had been around His head, not lying with the linen cloths, but folded together in a place by itself.

6. **Genesis 1:1-3** — In the beginning God created the heavens and the earth. The earth was without form, and void; and darkness was on the face of the deep. And the Spirit of God was hovering over the face of the waters. Then God said, "Let there be light"; and there was light.

7. **2 Corinthians 4:7** — But we have this treasure in earthen vessels, that the excellence of the power may be of God and not of us.

SYNOPSIS

There is nothing more powerful in this universe than the love of God. He loved us so much that He sent Jesus, who left the glory of Heaven to come to earth as a humble servant to die on the Cross for our sin. It is this love — the love of God — that brings order to our lives in the form of healing, peace, forgiveness, and everything we need to be victorious in this life.

The emphasis of this lesson:

God's love is the answer for everything we need in this life. His love casts out fear, gives purpose to our life, and equips us to love and bless others. It heals us, restores us, and provides for us completely. Whatever is out of order in our lives, He brings back into perfect order. His love never fails!

The Bible says that the love of God is not that we loved God, but that God loved us (*see* 1 John 4:10). He is perfect, wonderful, and more than we can even think or imagine. It does not matter what we think about ourselves, if we messed up, or who may have accused us. The love of God is stretched out for each one of us. His love never fails. He is wonderful!

God's Love Is the Answer

First John 4:8 says, "He who does not love does not know God, for God is love." Love is unfailing because love *is* God. God does not fail and neither does His love. First Corinthians 13:8 declares, "Love never fails…." We can go through all kinds of things in our life, and we will be tempted. The Bible says that offenses, tribulation, and trials will come (*see* John 16:33), but our response to adverse circumstances must be with the love of God.

The love of God never fails. His love is the highest thing that can be attained on Earth. It's not about our status, our popularity, or how many "likes" we get on social media. It's not about how successful we are in business or even in ministry. It is about the love of God that is manifest and shown through our life. "And now abide faith, hope, love, these three; but the greatest of these is love" (1 Corinthians 13:13). The highest of the highest is the love of God.

It's important to note that there are different kinds of love, and each kind of love is very different from the others. We're not referring to the love between friends, the love between family members, or even the love between a husband and wife. These are all wonderful. But we're focused on the love of God that dwells in our heart. When we became born again, the love of God came into our heart. *That's* the kind of love we're talking about.

Order Is Important to God

Hebrews 1:10-12 reveals something quite amazing about Jesus. This passage of scripture says, "You, Lord, in the beginning laid the foundation of the earth, and the heavens are the work of Your hands. They will perish, but You remain; and they will all grow old like a garment; like a cloak You will fold them up, and they will be changed. But You are the same, and Your years will not fail."

Jesus made everything. And there will be a time when everything He made perishes, but He will remain. On that day, He's going to take this earth like a garment, and God's going to fold it up. This passage may remind you of another scripture, which says,

> **And he [the apostle John], stooping down and looking in, saw the linen cloths lying there; yet he did not go in. Then Simon Peter came, following him, and went into the tomb; and he saw the linen cloths lying there, and the handkerchief that had been around His head, not lying with the linen cloths, but folded together in a place by itself.**
>
> **—John 20:5-7**

In this passage, Jesus has risen from the dead and the disciples have come to see where He was laid. The apostle John stooped down, looked into the tomb, and saw the linen burial cloths lying there, but he didn't go in. Then Simon Peter went into the tomb and "saw the linen cloths lying there, and the handkerchief that had been around His head, not lying with the linen cloths, but folded together in a place by itself."

Denise shared in her program that many years ago she struggled with housekeeping; she confessed she wasn't a good housekeeper. But through a series of events, God spoke to her heart about order and led her to these verses. She saw that order was very important to God. So much so that when Jesus rose from the dead, He even took the handkerchief that was placed around His head for burial, and He folded it neatly and laid it aside.

Jesus, the Son of God, had just risen from the dead. Yet He stopped to take the burial cloth from around His head and fold it. He could have just thrown it to the side, but He didn't. He placed it neatly in its own spot. How much does that say about the importance He places on order?

The Love of God Brings Order

It's the love of God that brings order. One day, Jesus is going to take this earth like a garment, and He's not just going to throw it to the side. In Hebrews 1:10-12, we see order. It says that one day, He will take His creation — the heavens and the earth — and, "like a cloak," He will "fold them up." God brings order.

When the things of this world (such as fear) attack us, what does love do? Love brings order because God is love, and God brings order. We see it is important to God not to just throw something aside but to bring order to it. We see this great love of our God bringing order in Genesis 1:1-3, which says,

> **In the beginning God created the heavens and the earth. The earth was without form, and void; and darkness was on the face of the deep. And the Spirit of God was hovering over the face of the waters. Then God said, "Let there be light"; and there was light.**

The earth was without form; it was chaos. But what happened? "The Spirit of God was hovering over the face of the waters" (Genesis 1:2). Here comes God! Here comes Love — bringing order to chaos. Then God said, "Let there be light," and there was light. He started bringing order.

First John 4:18 says, "There is no fear in love; but perfect love casts out fear, because fear involves torment. But he who fears has not been made perfect in love." The words "casts out" here mean *drives out* and indicate *the disciplinary action and chastisement of a wrongdoer.* Love *drives out* fear because fear is out of order. Fear brings torment, but love brings things into order.

Imagine that a rat got into your home. You would yell, "Get out right now! Get out!" And you would drive out that rat by any means available. That's a picture of what it means to cast out fear. God is love, and that Love lives in us. His perfect love that lives within us *drives out* fear and brings us back into order.

Love Brings Order to Our Mind, Body, and Emotions

It is God's perfect love that is recorded in Hebrews 1:10-12, when He declared, in essence, "I'm not going to just throw aside the earth. No, I'm going to take it into My hands and fold it." And when Jesus was raised from the dead, He didn't say, "I'm just going to throw this head covering to the side." No, He said, in effect, "I'm going to fold it up, and I'm going to bring order." The love of God never fails. It brings order to our disorder. The love of God casts out fear and brings back order to our mind, emotions, and body.

What about sickness? Sickness is definitely out of order, but Jesus took all of our sickness and disease on His own body. Think of cancer. Cancer is a disease of mutated cells that are out of order. But Jesus took cancer upon Himself and took it to the Cross. He took every disease that could come upon our bodies, and He brought order back to our bodies. He healed us. He took the punishment for sickness and disease on His own body so we could be healed. Fear tried to come upon Jesus that day, but He cast it out. God's perfect love drove out fear, and He brought it back in order.

Sin came to man, but God sent Jesus. Man was separated, and out of order from God, but Jesus came — Love came — and He put it back in order. What about divorce? It's out of order. And the Word of God gives us the order needed. Spouses are instructed, "Let each one of you in particular so love his own wife as himself, and let the wife see that she respects her husband" (Ephesians 5:33). This is perfect order. God is love, and His love places things back in order.

We Have This Treasure on the Inside

What about you? What kind of mess were you in before you were saved? Were you "out of order"? Maybe you were dealing with an addiction or a mean streak in your personality. Maybe you were judgmental or selfish or confronting fear and past hurts.

And then the Lover, Jesus, came! He disrupted that disorder through His love, and He brought you into perfect order with Himself. In your spirit, you are in perfect order with God. You're blameless. The Bible says you are above reproach in His sight (*see* Colossians 1:22). You're holy and beloved (*see* Colossians 3:12). You are the elect of God (*see* Romans 8:28-30). On the inside of you, you're absolutely perfect (*see* Ephesians 1:4,5).

Second Corinthians 4:7 says, "But we have this treasure in earthen vessels, that the excellence of the power may be of God and not of us." Is your body perfect? No. Is your mind perfect? No. Are your emotions perfect? No. But the Treasure who lives inside you is absolute perfection.

If you have made Jesus the Lord of your life, His Spirit lives within you, so you're in perfect order with God.

His Love Lacks Nothing

This perfect order is evident everywhere in creation. Have you ever looked at the order that can be seen in a flower? It's amazing! And what about the universe? What about the sun? Scientists say that if the sun was even a tiny bit closer to the Earth, the Earth would burn up. And if it was a little farther from the Earth, it would freeze. Who created that order? God did — *Love* did! The One who puts everything back in order, and he did that for you.

God is a God of order, and He established that perfect order inside you when He placed the Holy Spirit in you when you were born again. You're not lacking anything in your spirit. You have everything you need from Him — *absolutely everything*. He's put everything in order.

In Him, You Have All You Need

God put love in you. He put peace, long-suffering, patience, kindness, and gentleness in you. He has placed His love inside you and brought order to your life with the Holy Spirit — just as He did in Genesis. The earth was in chaos, but then the Spirit of God came over that chaos, and He began to speak. He said, "Let there be light" (Genesis 1:3), and He put everything in order.

If something is out of order, God brings order with His perfect love. The Love that brought order to the earth is also in you. It's encouraging to know that God is with you no matter what's happening around you. He is the One who has ordered everything perfectly inside you — order to your mind, your thoughts, and your emotions. Receive that today. Acknowledge it, and let His love start to restore order to your heart and mind. His perfect, unfailing love is within you!

STUDY QUESTIONS

Be diligent to present yourself approved to God, a worker who does not need to be ashamed, rightly dividing the word of truth.
— 2 Timothy 2:15

1. Read Mark 4:35-41. Jesus brought peace, tranquility, and order to this turbulent situation. How can you follow Jesus' example to see the storms in *your* life cease and calm restored? Is there an area of your life you need to address and say with authority, "Peace, be still"?

2. According to First John 3:14, how do we know we have passed from death to life?

3. The love of God never fails. It brings order to our disorder, casts out fear, and brings peace to our mind and emotions. What promises do we find in His Word about our mind and soul? (*Consider* Psalm 23:3; 2 Timothy 1:7; 1 Corinthians 2:16; and 3 John 2.)

PRACTICAL APPLICATION

But be doers of the word,
and not hearers only, deceiving yourselves.
—James 1:22

1. The Bible says that you will face offenses, tribulations, and trials in your life (*see* John 16:33). But how will you respond? You must answer with the love of God, because love never fails (*see* 1 Corinthians 13:8). Is there a circumstance you are currently facing? Yield to His love. Be an expression of His love and watch how He turns it around and "never fails." Thank Him now, in advance, for victory in that situation. Glory to God!

2. If you have never received Jesus as your Lord and Savior, today is the day of salvation. "If you confess with your mouth the Lord Jesus and believe in your heart that God has raised Him from the dead, you will be saved" (Romans 10:9). Allow God to bring order to your life as you receive His greatest gift — Jesus. Pray, *Father, I believe Jesus died on the Cross for my sins and rose from the dead, triumphing over all. Jesus, be my Lord. Thank You for saving me. Bring order into my life now in every area. In Jesus' name. Amen.*

3. Jesus took all sickness and every disease. He paid the price to bring order back to your physical body. If you are fighting symptoms, read Psalm 103:1-3; Isaiah 53:4,5; and First Peter 2:24. Pray, *Father, thank You for sending Jesus to pay the price for my sins and any sickness that would come against me. I believe I receive healing for my body from the top of my head to the soles of my feet, and I thank You for bringing order, peace, and wholeness to my entire body. In the mighty name of Jesus. Amen.*

Notes

CLAIM YOUR FREE RESOURCE!

As a way of introducing you further to the teaching ministry of Rick Renner, we would like to send you FREE of charge his teaching, "How To Receive a Miraculous Touch From God" on CD or as an MP3 download.

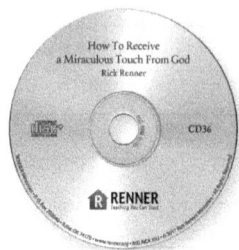

In His earthly ministry, Jesus commonly healed *all* who were sick of *all* their diseases. In this profound message, learn about the manifold dimensions of Christ's wisdom, goodness, power, and love toward all humanity who came to Him in faith with their needs.

☑ **YES, I want to receive Rick Renner's monthly teaching letter!**

Simply scan the QR code to claim this resource or go to: **renner.org/claim-your-free-offer**

Connect

WITH US!

renner.org

facebook.com/rickrenner • facebook.com/rennerdenise

youtube.com/rennerministries • youtube.com/deniserenner

instagram.com/rickrrenner • instagram.com/rennerministries_
instagram.com/rennerdenise

www.ingramcontent.com/pod-product-compliance
Lightning Source LLC
Chambersburg PA
CBHW071652040426
42452CB00009B/1845